10,000 *facts about* PEOPLE

DEE TURNER

Kingfisher Books

NEW YORK

Contents

KINGFISHER BOOKS
Grisewood & Dempsey Inc.
95 Madison Avenue
New York, New York 10016

First American edition 1992
10 9 8 7 6 5 4 3

Copyright © Times Four Publishing Ltd. 1992

ISBN 1-85697-810-9

Library of Congress Cataloging-in-Publication Data
Turner, Dee.
  People/Dee Turner. — 1st American ed.
    p. cm. — (1000 facts about)
  Includes index.
  1. Children's encyclopedias and dictionaries.
  2. Man — Juvenile literature. I. Title. II. Series
PZ7.S966Mi 1993   92-53102 CIP AC

Produced by Times Four Publishing Ltd.
Designed by Brian Robertson
Cover design by Terry Woodley
Illustrated by Peter Bull, Shelagh McNicholas, Guy Smith, Michael Steward
Printed in Spain

Introduction

This book gives you some fascinating insights into a most remarkable creature — the human being. Find out, for example, how human bodies are made and how they work. Discover how people communicate with each other, what they believe in, what pastimes they enjoy, and how they live.

Read, too, about many of the things people have been able to create — from paintings, literature, and music to machines that have transformed the world and sent humans traveling into space.

Also, there are lots of easy-to-find facts beginning with a spot, like this:

● By the time they are two years old, most children can use several hundred words.

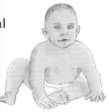

Across the top of each page there is a list of useful mini-facts — for example, what the human body is made of, some unusual foods from around the world, or when and where some of the world's most popular games were invented.

On each double page there is a Strange but True section containing some unusual or startling facts.

On pages 42-45 you will find charts and lists of records and facts about people.

If you are not sure where to find out about a particular topic, look in the Index on pages 46-48.

To help you pick out the things you want to read about, some key words are in bold type like this: **Olympic Games**.

The first recognizable **human beings** probably appeared about 2 million years ago, although groups of human-like creatures existed before then. People looking similar to ourselves have lived on Earth for only about 100,000 years — which is just a fraction of time in the history of the Earth.

The first humans

Scientists studying **fossils** of bones and other remains have managed to piece together some idea of what the **first humans** were like.

Australopithecines

- About 3.5 million years ago, Australopithecines lived in Africa. They had apelike faces but walked upright and probably used sticks and pieces of bone as tools.

Neanderthal skull

Modern skull

- About 2 million years ago, creatures called Homo Habilis (handy man) lived in Africa. They had larger brains than Australopithecines. They sharpened stones to make tools, built shelters, and worked together to hunt animals.

Homo Habilis

- About 1.6 million years ago Homo Erectus (upright man) appeared, first in Africa then also spreading to Asia. These people were taller than Homo Habilis, with larger brains. They used many different stone tools and discovered how to use fire for cooking and keeping warm.

Homo Erectus

- About 200,000 to 100,000 years ago Homo Sapiens (thinking man) appeared. People today belong to this group. The Neanderthal people were an early kind of Homo Sapiens. They lived in caves in Europe 60,000 years ago, wore animal skins and made carvings of animals.

A Neanderthal man

Strange but true

- The axes in use today are very like some of the earliest hunting weapons.

- About 1 million years ago, some humans built huts from mammoth bones covered over with animal skins.

- Early humans may have learned to cook meat by accidentally dropping it onto a fire.

- The human being's nearest animal relatives are thought to be gorillas, chimpanzees, and orangutans.

4

The first modern people

The Neanderthal people gradually died out, but by this time other types of **Homo Sapiens** had developed and spread around the world. These are some of the things the **first modern humans** did:

● Decorated tools with pictures of animals and painted hunting scenes on the walls of their cave homes.

● Made jewelry from shells and animal teeth, and clothes from skins sewn together with needles made of bone.

● Buried their dead, painting the bodies red and putting tools and weapons in the graves. This may have been part of a religious ceremony, showing belief in life after death.

The first farmers

At first, people lived as **nomads**, which means they wandered around in small groups or tribes searching for good hunting grounds. About 10,000 years ago an important change took place. People living in the Middle East began to settle down and farm. These **first farmers** learned how to:

● Sow seeds and grow crops.

● Capture wild goats and sheep and breed them to provide people with milk, meat, and skins.

● Build houses of mud and straw that dried hard in the sun.

● Bake bread in ovens. Early bread was flat and hard.

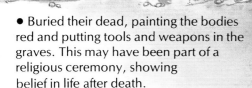

Towns and trading

When people settled in groups or communities, they sometimes produced more goods than they needed for themselves. So they began to **trade** their extra goods for other things made by people nearby. Gradually, towns grew in size and became busy **trading centers**.

● People living in settled farming communities had more time to develop skills such as pottery, weaving, and toolmaking.

● Eventually, some people became craftworkers, specializing in making certain goods to sell.

● Before money was invented, people bartered (exchanged) their goods. People with spare wheat, for example, might swap it with someone else for pottery or wool.

Weaving at a loom

People of the World

For thousands of years the **number of people** living on Earth increased very slowly. Early peoples lived **shorter lives** than most people do today. Very little was known about **medicine**, so many people died from illness or injury before they reached old age.

Today, in many countries people are better housed and fed and there are **medical services** to take care of illness, so people live longer. As a result, the number of people in the world has grown rapidly.

B.C. and A.D.

The letters B.C. after a number mean the years before the birth of Christ. A.D. stands for the Latin words *anno domini* (year of Our Lord) and means a date after the birth of Christ.

● B.C. numbers count backward, so (for example) 1000 B.C. is further back in time than 500 B.C.

How cities have grown

These are the populations of some of the world's largest **cities**, now and in the past:

The population explosion

About 155 people are born every minute of every day. This recent rise in population is often called the **population explosion**. If this rate of growth continues, the world population will have trebled by the end of the next century.

● World population grew much more slowly in the past. It took about 11,500 years for it to grow from 10 million to 500 million. Since 1800 it has grown very quickly.

This diagram shows how the population has increased over the last thousand years.

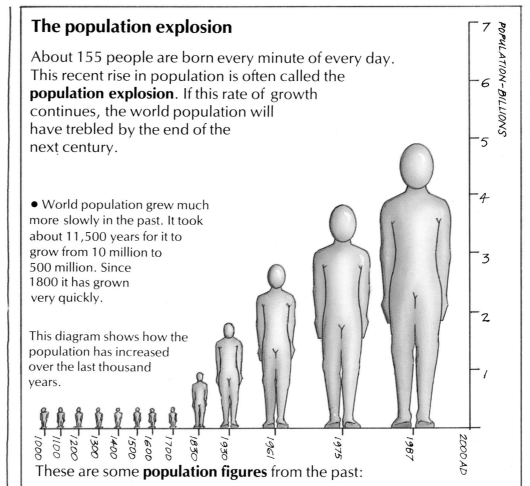

These are some **population figures** from the past:

● In 8000 B.C. there were probably only about 6 million people in the world. Most lived in Asia and Africa.

● By A.D. 1, people had spread to most parts of the world. The population had grown to about 255 million.

● By 1600 the world population had doubled to about 500 million.

● In 1987 the world population rose to 5 billion, ten times as many people as in 1600. About three-fourths of the world's people today live in Asia and Europe.

● At its present rate of growth, the world population doubles about every 40 years.

Rome

Jericho

● 27,000 B.C.: The city of Dolní Vestonice (in modern Czechoslovakia) contained about 100 people

● 7800 B.C.: Jericho (now in occupied Jordan) contained about 27,000 people

● As early as 133 B.C., Rome was a huge city with a million inhabitants

Great Britain:
75 years

U.S.A.:
76 years

Ethiopia:
52 years

Strange but true

- The Chinese population is increasing at 35,000 a day — over 12 million a year!

- At present, one person in three is under 15 years of age. Fewer than one person in ten is over 64 years of age.

- It is estimated that the average length of life in A.D. 400 was about 33 years for a man and 27 for a woman.

Population problems

The rapid rise in population has created many **problems**:

- Shortage of food. To feed everyone, we will have to produce more food and share it out more fairly.

- Pollution due to the increased use of fuels. Supplies of oil, coal, and gas are also running low and cannot be replaced.

- Destruction of wildlife habitats for housing, industry, and farming.

- Widespread poverty and hunger, especially in Africa and Asia.

- Shortage of housing.

- Unemployment.

Countries

At present, the world is divided into about 170 **independent countries**. This number keeps changing, as countries join together or become separate.

- An independent country is one that has its own government, makes its own laws and has its own flag.

Vatican City

- The smallest independent country is the Vatican City in Rome. It is an area of 109 acres (0.4 sq-km) governed by the Roman Catholic Church.

- The country with the highest population is China, with over 1 billion people living there.

- In these countries most people live in towns or cities: UK 91%, Australia 85%, U.S.A. and Japan 76%. In these countries, most people live and work in farming: India 72%, Kenya 80% and Burkino Faso (Africa) 91%.

London

- London did not have one million inhabitants until 1800. Now it has over 6 million

Tokyo

- Some modern cities:
1985: Mexico City, 8.8 million
1989: Tokyo, Japan, 8.2 million
1988: New York, 7.3 million
1989: Shanghai, China, 7.2 million

The **human body** is made up of many different parts, including billions of **cells**, thousands of miles of **tubing**, and hundreds of **muscles** and **bones**. Each of the many different parts of the body has its own special job, but all the parts have to work together to keep the body alive.

Strange but true

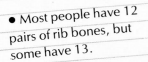

- The hair on your head usually lives for 2 to 6 years before dropping out. Eyelash hairs last for only about 10 weeks.

- Most people have 12 pairs of rib bones, but some have 13.

- On average, a human being eats 50 tons of food and drinks 13,000 gallons (50,000 liters) of liquid in a lifetime.

- Each person walks about 15,000 miles (25,000 km) during a lifetime.

Cells

Everything in the body is made up of tiny living units called **cells**. A fully grown body has about **50 billion cells**.

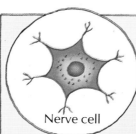

Nerve cell

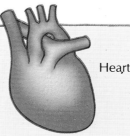

Heart

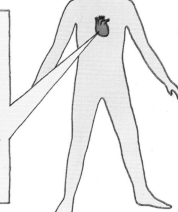

Heart position

- A group of similar cells doing the same job is called tissue. Muscles and nerves are tissues.

- Different types of tissue working together form organs, such as the heart and the lungs.

The skeleton

The **skeleton** is a framework, made of about **206 bones**, that supports the body, gives it shape, and protects it from damage.

- The skull protects the brain and the ribs protect the heart.

- Joints are where two bones meet. Some are fixed but others can bend.

Movable knee joint

Skeleton

Muscles

The human body has about **650 muscles**. They enable the skeleton to **move**.

- Muscles move by contracting (tensing) or relaxing (loosening). They are joined to bones by fibers. When muscles contract, the fibers pull the bones and make them move. Most muscles work in pairs, pulling opposite ways.

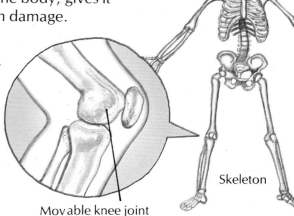

Tensed muscle

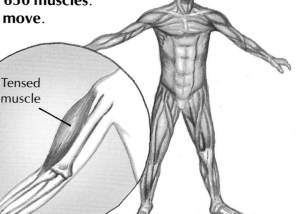

Body muscles

The blood system

Blood carries **oxygen gas** and dissolved food particles called **nutrients** to all the cells in the body, so that they can make **energy**.

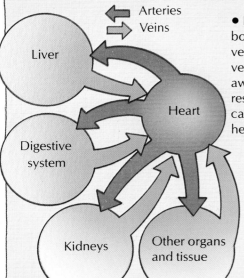

Arteries
Veins

Liver

Heart

Digestive system

Kidneys

Other organs and tissue

● Blood flows around the body in tubes called vessels. Arteries are blood vessels that carry blood away from the heart to the rest of the body. Veins carry blood back to the heart.

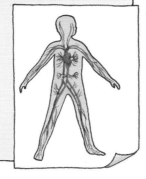

The lungs

Oxygen passes into the blood through the lung walls when we breathe in. Waste **carbon dioxide** gas is passed back into the lungs from the blood.

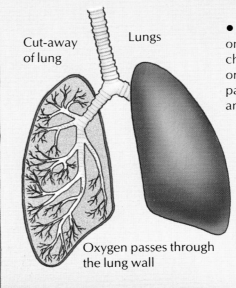

Cut-away of lung

Lungs

Oxygen passes through the lung wall

● There are two lungs, one in each side of the chest. They are spongy organs made of tightly packed tissue, nerves, and blood vessels.

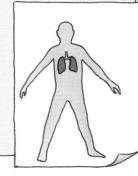

The digestive system

Everything a human being eats has to be broken down by the body before **nutrients** from the food can be taken into the blood and turned into energy.

This process takes place in the **digestive system**, a series of connected parts that make up a passage beginning at the mouth and ending at the anus.

1. Food goes down the throat into the stomach, where chemicals called digestive juices break it down.

2. The food passes on to the small intestine (about 20 feet (6m) long), where most digestion takes place.

3. Nutrients pass through the intestine wall. They are carried by the blood to the liver, which stores them or sends them where they are needed.

4. The food goes into the large intestine. If there is any water or other useful substance left, they pass into the blood through the intestine wall.

5. The kidneys filter out liquid waste called urine. It is stored in the bladder until you go to the toilet.

6. Solid waste is stored in the rectum at the end of the intestine. It leaves your body through the anus as feces.

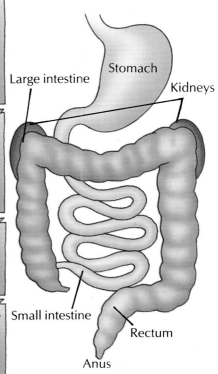

Large intestine

Stomach

Kidneys

Small intestine

Rectum

Anus

9

Body Controls

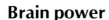

The human body has a very efficient system for **sensing** the world around it. It can feel, see, hear, smell, and taste things and deal with all this information better than any computer. It has to do this to survive.

All the information the body receives is processed by the **brain**, which is more highly developed in humans than in any other animal species.

Brain power

The **brain** is the body's **control center**. It keeps the body running smoothly, thinks and makes decisions, stores memories, and produces feelings such as happiness, anger, and sorrow.

● The body is continually sending messages to the brain telling it what is happening. The brain sends messages back telling the body parts what to do. The messages pass along nerves that run throughout the body.

Nerves

Spinal cord section

● Nerves work rather like telephone wires, carrying information in the form of tiny electrical signals.

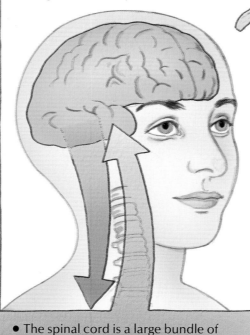

● The spinal cord is a large bundle of nerves that runs from the brain down the back, inside the bones that make up the spine. Smaller nerves run from the spinal cord to the rest of the body. Messages travel up and down the spinal cord.

● The brain gets messages about the world outside the body from the senses. People have five main senses — sight, hearing, smell, taste, and touch. The sense organs are the body parts that sense things. They are the eyes, ears, nose, tongue, and skin.

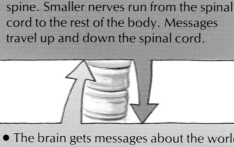
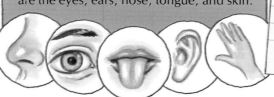
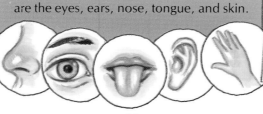

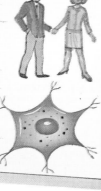

Strange but true

● An adult's brain weighs about 3 pounds (1.4 kg). It is roughly the shape of a cauliflower.

● The body's fastest messages pass along the nerves at 250 mph (400km/h).

● Very few women are color-blind, but on average 1 in 12 men cannot see some colors properly.

● One brain cell may be connected to as many as 25,000 other brain cells.

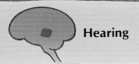 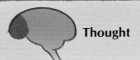
Seeing

The **eye** has a special lining called the **retina**. This contains cells that are sensitive to light. Messages from these cells pass along **nerves** to the **brain**, which works out what the eyes are looking at.

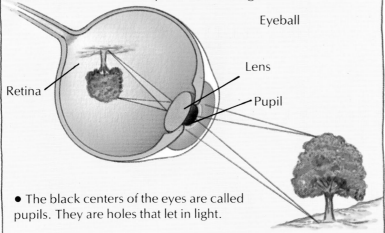

Eyeball

Lens

Pupil

Retina

● The black centers of the eyes are called pupils. They are holes that let in light.

● Behind the pupil is a lens. It focuses light rays into an upside-down picture on the retina inside the back of the eyeball. The brain turns the image the right way up.

Hearing

The part of the ear you can see is called the **outer ear**. This collects and funnels sounds into the **inner ear**. Inside the inner ear:

● The sounds make the eardrum vibrate, or shake. The vibrations pass on through two small bones called the hammer and the anvil, and then through a group of three tiny bones called the stirrup.

Anvil

Hammer

Stirrup

Cochlea

Eardrum

● Finally the vibrations reach a coiled tube called the cochlea. This is filled with liquid and lined with tiny hairs connected to nerve-endings. These pass messages about the vibrations to the brain.

Smelling and tasting

Inside the back of the **nose** there are nerve-endings that pick up **smells** and send messages about them to the brain. On the **tongue**, special groups of cells called **tastebuds** pick up and send messages about **taste**.

● Tiny smell molecules travel through the air and enter the nasal cavity behind your nose.

Nasal cavity

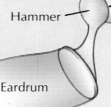

Magnified tastebud

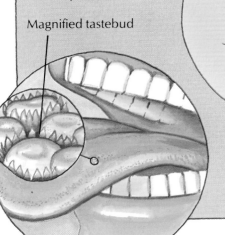

● Tastebuds can pick up four basic kinds of taste — bitter, sweet, sour, and salty.

Touching

Your **skin** is full of nerve-endings that supply the brain with information about **touch**. There are lots of different nerve-endings to pick up information about different kinds of touch sensations.

● A piece of skin the size of a small coin has at least 35 nerve-endings in it, as well as over 3 million cells, 3 feet (1m) of blood vessels and many tiny bundles of cells called glands, which produce sweat and oil.

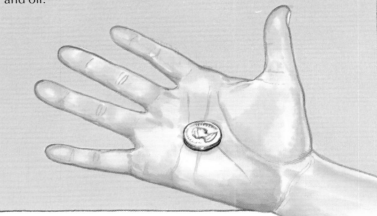

11

New Life

All new life begins with just one **cell**. To make this first cell, a male **sperm** must enter a female **egg** called an **ovum**. The cell then starts growing and dividing to make new cells. These divide in turn to make the millions of cells found in the human body. The creation of new life is called **reproduction**.

People grow and change throughout their lives, from birth to old age. No two human beings are exactly the same in looks or in personality, but everyone goes through the same stages of development.

How babies are born

The moment when a sperm enters an egg is called **conception** or **fertilization**.

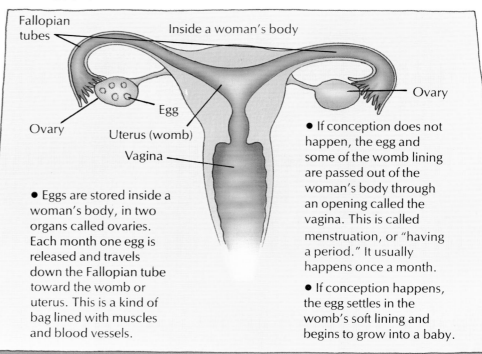

Fallopian tubes — Inside a woman's body

Ovary

Egg

Ovary

Uterus (womb)

Vagina

● Eggs are stored inside a woman's body, in two organs called ovaries. Each month one egg is released and travels down the Fallopian tube toward the womb or uterus. This is a kind of bag lined with muscles and blood vessels.

● If conception does not happen, the egg and some of the womb lining are passed out of the woman's body through an opening called the vagina. This is called menstruation, or "having a period." It usually happens once a month.

● If conception happens, the egg settles in the womb's soft lining and begins to grow into a baby.

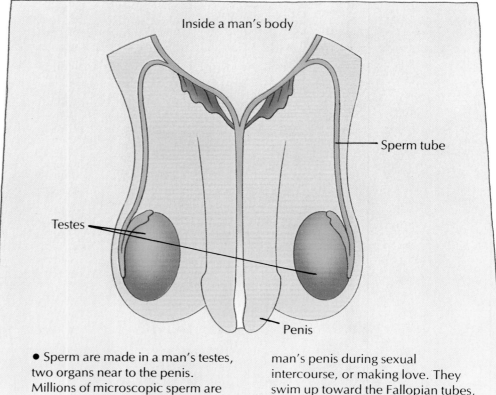

Inside a man's body

Sperm tube

Testes

Penis

● Sperm are made in a man's testes, two organs near to the penis. Millions of microscopic sperm are put into the woman's vagina by the man's penis during sexual intercourse, or making love. They swim up toward the Fallopian tubes, but only one enters the egg.

Strange but true

● Children tend to grow faster in spring and summer.

● On average, women tend to live longer than men.

● If you carried on growing as fast as a baby does in the womb, you would be 50 feet (15m) by the time your were 10 years old!

● The most babies born to a mother at one birth is 10.

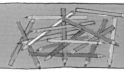
Iron: as much as in a 1 inch (2.5 cm-long) nail

Carbon: as much as in 9,000 pencils

Water: two-thirds of the body is water. Adults contain about 12 gallons (45l).

How babies grow

From **conception** to **birth** takes about 38 weeks. Here are some of the stages along the way:

- Six weeks: the baby is very small, about an inch (2.4 cm) long. It has begun to develop a nervous system, a heart, a digestive tract, and sense organs. It has buds that will develop into arms and legs.

- Twelve weeks: the baby is between 2½ and 3 inches (6.25 cm and 7.5 cm) long. It is inside a fluid-filled bag called the amniotic sac, connected to its mother by an umbilical cord.

- Twenty-eight weeks: the baby is between 12 and 14 inches (30 and 36 cm) long and weighs about 30 ounces (900 grams.) A creamy-colored wax has now developed over its body.

- Around 38 weeks: the baby is ready to be born. It is 20 inches (50 cm) long and weighs 6 to 11 pounds (3 to 5 kg).

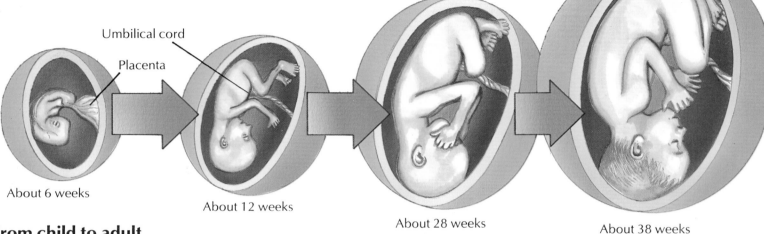

Umbilical cord

Placenta

About 6 weeks

About 12 weeks

About 28 weeks

About 38 weeks

From child to adult

The period of time when children are growing into adults is called **adolescence**. The early part of adolescence, when bodies change, is called **puberty**. The changes take place at any time between the ages of 10 and 15. Here are some of them:

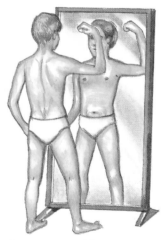

- Girls start to menstruate (have periods). Their breasts start to grow bigger, their hips get broader and they grow more body hair.

- Boys start making sperm in their testes. They grow facial hair and their voices "break" or deepen. Their shoulders and chests get broader.

Growing older

Once people are fully grown their bodies very slowly start to **wear out** and **slow down**.

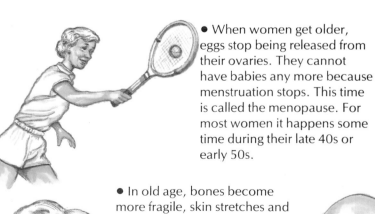

- When women get older, eggs stop being released from their ovaries. They cannot have babies any more because menstruation stops. This time is called the menopause. For most women it happens some time during their late 40s or early 50s.

- In old age, bones become more fragile, skin stretches and wrinkles, and hair often goes white and gets thinner. Muscles become weaker and some people cannot hear or see as well as they once could.

M ost people live in small groups called **families** that contain **parents**, **children**, and (sometimes) other **relatives**. One important purpose of the family is to look after its members. The aged and sick can be looked after by younger members of the family, and babies and young children can be cared for until they are old enough to look after themselves.

Not all families are the same. Here you can find out about some of the ways people live around the world.

Families

There are different **kinds of families**. Nuclear families are the most common kind, but there are many other family patterns.

● Nuclear family: a mother, father, and a child or children living together.

● Extended family: a large group of grandparents, parents, children, and other relatives all living together.

● Single-parent family: a child or children living with one parent only.

● Commune: a large group of people living together as a family, but not necessarily related.

● Clan or tribe: a large group made up of families that are related to each other.

Strange but true

● The custom of giving wedding rings dates back to ancient Roman times.

● An American man called Glynn Wolfe has been married a total of 27 times!

● Viking families always sent their children away to live with other people.

● 6,516 couples were married in the same mass ceremony in South Korea in 1988.

Marriage

Marriage is an agreement to live together made by a man and a woman. The **wedding** or **marriage** **ceremony** is important in many religions (see p.24). It is usually a time for **celebration**.

- In societies such as Australia, Canada, Europe, and the United States, most people are free to choose who they want to marry.

- In most societies, people have one marriage partner at a time. This is called monogamy.

- In a few societies, men can have more than one wife at a time. This is called polygamy.

- A common-law marriage is when a couple live together as husband and wife but do not go through a legal or religious marriage ceremony.

- Some married couples decide that they are not happy living together. In many societies they can end the marriage by getting divorced.

- In some places, such as India and the Middle East, parents choose marriage partners for their children.

Having babies

Different societies around the world have special **customs** for the birth of a baby:

- The Mbuti pygmies of the African rain forests tie a piece of jungle vine around a new baby's waist. They attach a small piece of wood to the vine to pass on the strength of the forest to the baby.

- The Ainu hunters of northern Japan make a tiny cut in a new baby's thigh. They dress the cut with fungi to pass on the magical power of sacred trees.

- The Nootka tribe, from the northwest coast of North America, believe that twins are magical. If a family has twins, the parents and children are kept apart from the rest of the tribe for four years, so their magical properties will develop.

- In many societies births are followed by a religious festival. In Christian countries babies are christened. They have the sign of the cross made on their foreheads with holy water.

Talking To Each Other

Although many creatures communicate with each other using sounds, only humans have developed **spoken language** to tell each other about their ideas and feelings.

There are about 5,000 languages in the world today, but many of them are spoken only by small groups of people. Most languages have variations or **dialects** – different forms of a language that are spoken only in particular areas.

People have tried to invent a new language that everyone in the world could share. The most successful so far is **Esperanto**, which more than 100 million people have learned since its invention in 1887.

Learning a language

Most young children learn the **language** spoken by their **family** very easily, almost without knowing they are doing so.

● Babies learn by listening to the voices they hear around them and by copying sounds and words.

● By the time they are two years old, most children can use several hundred words.

● Children who are brought up hearing two languages all the time soon learn to speak both. Someone who speaks two languages is called bilingual.

Languages

Languages are divided into groups, called **families**. All the languages in a family developed from one earlier language.

● About 48% (almost half the world's people) speak a language from the Indo-European family. This includes all the major languages of Europe as well as some from Iran and India.

● About 23% (nearly a quarter of the world's people) speak one of the Chinese family of languages.

mat (Russian)
meter (Greek)
madre (Spanish)
mutter (Germany)
mère (French)
mother (English)

● Here are some words for "mother" in Indo-European languages. They all come from the word *mata*, which is "mother" in the ancient Sanskrit language.

Changing languages

Languages change all the time. Words may be **borrowed** from other languages, or **invented** to name a new idea or object.

● Many English words have been invented. For example, the word *television* was invented using *tele* (a Greek word meaning "far") and *vision* (from the Latin word for "to see").

● These English words were borrowed: *Mosquito* (Spanish), *Tea* (Chinese), *Sugar* (Arabic), *Shampoo* (Hindi), *Ski* (Norwegian), *Robot* (Czech), *Ketchup* (Malay), *Parka* (Russian).

Writing things down

Writing developed much later than spoken language. Here are some facts about **written languages**:

Hieroglyph examples

Greek alphabet

αβßγδεζηθικλμνξπορσςτυφφχψω ΑΒΓΔΕΖΗΘΙΚΛΜΝΞΟΠΡΣΤΥΦ ΧΨΩ 1234567890 .,:;

Arabic alphabet

ابتثجحخدذرزسشصضطظعغفقكلمنهوىلا
١٢٣٤٥٦٧٨٩٠

Chinese symbols

生 拿 個
火. 你 燈

- The first written languages used picture symbols to represent whole words.

- The earliest-known picture symbols were used in the Iranian region in about 3500 B.C. The Ancient Egyptians began using picture symbols called hieroglyphics in about 3000 B.C.

- Most modern languages are written in alphabets. The words are spelled out with letters. Each letter represents a sound.

- The Phoenicians, who lived along the Mediterranean, developed the first alphabet in about 1000 B.C.

- Chinese is the only major modern language that has no alphabet. Instead it has around 50,000 picture symbols.

- Some Chinese words are made from one symbol. Others are made up of various symbols mixed together.

Speaking without words

Movements made by the face, head, arms, hands, and body can signal thoughts and feelings almost as clearly as spoken words. These signals are called **body language**.

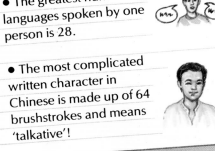
- When people are nervous they often fidget with their hands.

- The distance between people who are talking to each other is important. If one person stands too close, the other one may feel threatened and move away.

- Body language varies from place to place. For example, in some countries looking a person straight in the eye means that you are honest and truthful. In other countries it is regarded as bad manners.

Food

Without food, people cannot survive. Food gives the body **energy** to make it work.

To stay healthy, you need a **balanced diet**: a good mixture of the different kinds of food available. Sadly, many people in the world today do not have enough food to eat.

Meal with animal products

Vegetarian meal

All food comes from plants or animals. Humans are **omnivorous**, which means they are able to eat both meat and plants. However, some people choose to be **vegetarian**, which means they do not eat meat.

Plant food

Plants that grow well in a particular part of the world provide the **staple diet**, or main food, of that area. Here are some staple foods and the places where they are eaten:

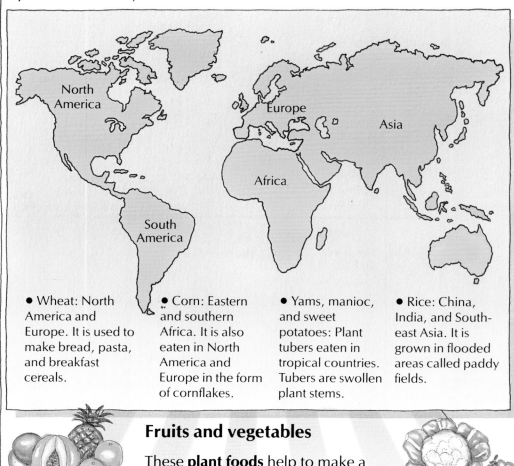

- Wheat: North America and Europe. It is used to make bread, pasta, and breakfast cereals.

- Corn: Eastern and southern Africa. It is also eaten in North America and Europe in the form of cornflakes.

- Yams, manioc, and sweet potatoes: Plant tubers eaten in tropical countries. Tubers are swollen plant stems.

- Rice: China, India, and Southeast Asia. It is grown in flooded areas called paddy fields.

Fruits and vegetables

These **plant foods** help to make a healthy diet:

- Fruit contains a plant's seeds. Many fruits are sweet and juicy.

- Vegetables come from different plant parts. Here are some examples:

ROOTS: carrots, beetroot, and parsnips

LEAVES: lettuce and spinach

STALKS: celery and asparagus

BUDS: cabbage and brussels sprouts

SEEDS: peas, beans, and sweet corn

FLOWERS: cauliflower

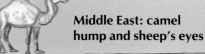
What food contains

Food contains **nutrients**, which the body needs to keep it healthy. Here are the main nutrients, what they do, and a list of some of the foods in which they are found:

Nutrients	What They Do	Where Found
Proteins	Help the body cells to grow and repair injuries	Meat, fish, cheese, eggs, beans
Carbohydrates	Provide energy	Bread, potatoes, pasta, rice, flour, sugar
Fats	Build body cells and provide energy	Milk, cheese, oils, butter, oily fish, nuts
Vitamins	Keep the body healthy	There are about 20 vitamins, found in many different foods. Vitamin C, for example, is found in fruit and vegetables
Minerals	Many minerals are found in food, including calcium (builds teeth and bone) and iron (keeps blood healthy)	Cheese, milk (calcium) Liver, brown bread (iron)

Cooking food

The first humans ate their food raw. Then, about 500,000 years ago, people learned how to use fire for **cooking**. This is what cooking does:

● Breaks down tough food so that you can eat and digest it more easily. Cooking different foods together creates new tastes.

● Helps to preserve food from going rotten. It also destroys some nutrients, so vegetables and fruit are sometimes better for you if eaten raw.

Strange but true

● The longest sausage ever made was 13 miles (21 km) long – enough to reach to the top of the world's tallest building 44 times.

● Kebabs (meat cooked on skewers) were invented by Turkish soldiers who spiked meat onto their swords to roast in a fire.

● The first plates were simply large pieces of bread that you ate along with the meal.

Clothes

Human beings are the only creatures that wear **clothes**. People need clothes because, unlike most other animals, they have no **fur or feathers** to protect them.

The earliest people wore simple clothes made of **animal skins** to protect their bodies. Over the years people began to use clothes for decoration as well as for comfort.

Clothes can tell you something about a person — for instance, which part of the world they come from, or what work they do.

Making clothes

Over thousands of years, humans have developed **tools** for making clothes and have learned how to make and use lots of different **fabrics** (materials).

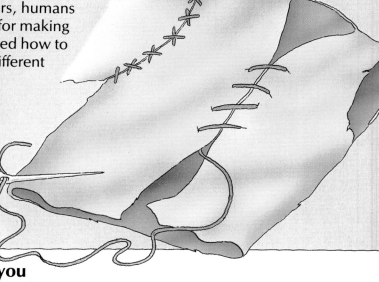

- The first needles were made of bone. They were used about 40,000 years ago.

- The first sewing thread was made from narrow strips of leather.

What clothes tell you

Clothes can sometimes tell you what **work** people do or what **group** they belong to. Here are some examples of this:

- To show wealth and power: rulers such as kings and queens sometimes wear robes and crowns to show their power.

- For protection at work: astronauts, firefighters, and surgeons all wear special clothing to protect their bodies.

- To show membership of a group: sports teams wear uniforms; fans wear the team's colors.

- To show authority: police, soldiers, pilots, ships' officers, and many others wear uniforms that people can identify.

20

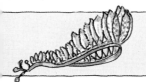 **North America: Native American headdress**

 **Hawaii: grass skirt and flowers**

 **Africa: tribal celebration dress**

- The fluffy fibers produced by the cotton plant are spun together and woven to make cotton fabric. People first learned how to make cotton cloth about 5,000 years ago.

- Chinese people have been making silk for over 4,000 years. Silk is made by unwinding the cocoons of silk moths and spinning the thread into soft fabric.

- The first sewing machines came into use in the 1850s.

- Wool is made by spinning the fleece of sheep. It used to be done on spinning wheels.

Fashion

Fashion is a **style of dressing** followed by a group of people. Here are some of the ways European men and women have dressed in the past:

- About 600 years ago, men and women wore long robes.

- About 500 years ago, many men wore doublets (jackets with a padded chest) and hose (leggings).

- Long pants for men did not appear until about 1830. Women did not wear pants regularly until about 1940.

- Today, many boys and girls wear the same kinds of clothes. Jeans and t-shirts are popular in many countries.

1300

1500

1850

1990

Climate

Clothes are designed to keep people warm or keep them cool, according to the **climate**.

- In the freezing Arctic areas of Canada, Greenland, and Russia, people wear layers of thick padded clothing to keep warm.

- In many hot countries, people wear long cool robes to protect them from the Sun.

Homes

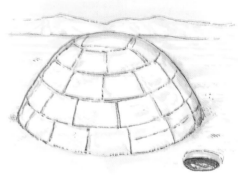

People need **homes** where they can eat, sleep, and shelter from the weather. Most houses are made of materials that are easy to find in the place where they are built. They are usually designed to suit the **climate** of their area.

In some countries people build their own homes. In other countries, architects design houses and builders construct them.

Shapes and sizes

Here are some traditional house styles from around the world, built to suit the **climate** and local **materials**.

- Iceland: turf roofs are used to keep the heat in.

- Arctic: Inuit (Eskimo) people build temporary houses made of blocks of snow, called igloos.

Homes on the move

Nomads are people who have no fixed home. They move around looking for work or pastures for their animals.

Strange but true

- The world's largest palace has 1,788 rooms. It was built for the Sultan of Brunei.

- Toilets were not installed in most houses until the mid 1800s.

- The world's tallest apartment house is the Metropolitan Tower in New York. People live in the top 48 stories, with 30 office floors below.

Middle East: cave dwellings

Hong Kong: houseboat on the harbor

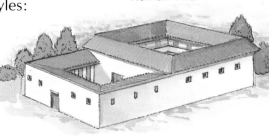
California: experimental house run on solar power

● South America: the Queche Indians build homes of mud bricks with thick pampas grass on the roof.

● Around the Mediterranean: many houses are painted white to reflect sunshine. Some have window shutters to keep the inside cool.

● Switzerland: houses have long sloping roofs so that snow can slide off them in winter.

● Asia: in marshy areas, people live in houses built on stilts to protect them from floods and wild animals.

● Big cities: land is scarce and expensive so buildings are built high into the air with lots of families living in each building.

● In the last century, American settlers lived in covered wagons as they traveled across the country to the West.

● In the Sahara Desert nomadic people live in tents made from cloth of woven goat hair. The sides can be rolled up to let cool breezes in.

● In Iran the Turkoman people live in circular tents made of wood and felt.

● In Siberia some nomadic people live in tents made of walrus skin.

Houses in the past

Here are some **ancient** house styles:

Dugout hut

Roman villa

● Prehistoric dugout hut (Europe: about 3000 B.C.).

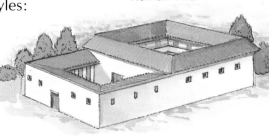

● Roman villa built around a courtyard (Europe: about 2,000 years ago).

● Half-timbered houses (parts of Northern Europe: 500 years ago).

Half-timbered houses

Religion

Religions are beliefs that are found all over the world. They have **rules of behavior** that their followers obey, and a **god** or **gods** that they worship. There are usually special **religious ceremonies** and **places of worship**.

Religion began thousands of years ago. Early humans explained natural events such as thunderstorms by saying that gods made them happen. People also made gods of the Sun, Moon, and Earth. They prayed to them for good hunting or crops.

Today, millions of people follow one or other of the major world religions.

World religions

These are the major **world religions**:

● Christianity: founded by Jesus Christ, whose birth nearly 2,000 years ago marks the beginning of the Christian calendar. Christians believe there is one God, and that Jesus Christ was God on Earth in human form. Their holy book is the Bible.

● Hinduism: developed in India at least 2,500 years ago. There are many gods, with Brahma as the most important. Hindus believe in reincarnation, which means that people are reborn many times. In each new life they are rewarded or punished for their deeds in an earlier life.

● Shinto: a Japanese religion whose followers believe that spirits are present in all living things. They worship at holy places called shrines.

An Anglican (Christian) bishop

Strange but true

● Archaeologists think that some caves in Europe were used as places of worship more than 14,000 years ago.

● The world's largest temple is Angkor Wat in Cambodia. It is over 1,000 years old.

● The largest recorded gathering of people was at a Hindu religious festival in India in 1989. It was attended by about 15 million people.

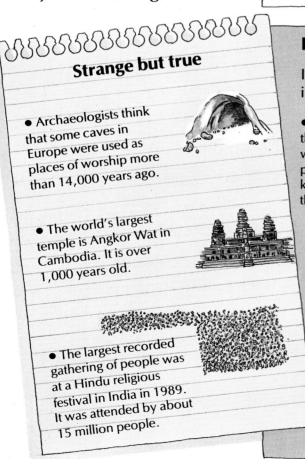

Holy objects

In all religions, **holy places** and **sacred objects** are an important part of worship.

● Copies of the Torah, the Jewish Holy Law, are written in Hebrew on parchment scrolls and kept in a casket called the Ark.

Jewish religious service

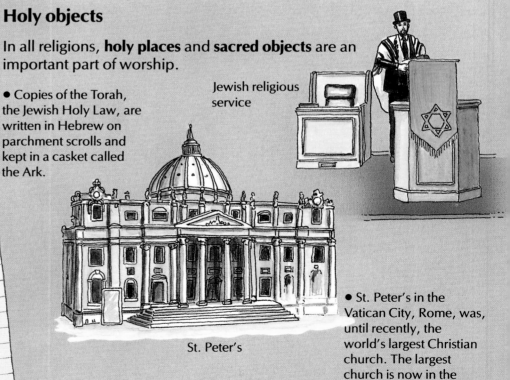

St. Peter's

● St. Peter's in the Vatican City, Rome, was, until recently, the world's largest Christian church. The largest church is now in the Ivory Coast, Africa. It was completed in 1989.

A Buddhist priest

- Buddhism: founded in India about 2,500 years ago by Siddhartha Gautama, who was given the title "Buddha." He said that people could escape suffering and find perfect peace ("nirvana") by following his teachings.

- Islam: the religion of Muslims — people who follow the teaching of Muhammad. It was founded nearly 1,400 years ago in the Middle East when the prophet Muhammad received messages from Allah (God). They were written down to form the Koran, the Islamic sacred book.

- Judaism: the religion of Jewish people, founded more than 4,000 years ago. Jews believe in one God who has chosen them to pass on his Commandments (laws) to the world. They believe a Messiah (savior) will come from God to bring peace to the world.

Odin

Ancient religions

- The Viking people of Scandinavia had many gods. The most important, Odin, rode an eight-legged horse. The gods lived in a paradise called Valhalla.

- Aztec people, who lived in Mexico about 800 years ago, worshiped many gods. They made human sacrifices by killing people and tearing out their hearts.

The Ka'bah in Mecca

- The Ka'bah in Mecca, Saudi Arabia, contains a sacred black stone. It is the most holy shrine of Islam. Many thousands of Muslims visit it each year.

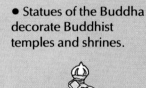

- Statues of the Buddha decorate Buddhist temples and shrines.

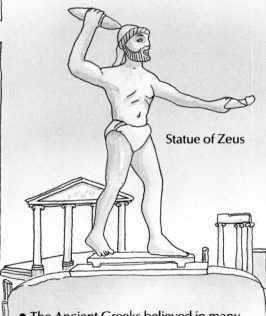

Statue of Zeus

- The Ancient Greeks believed in many gods and goddesses, who lived on Mount Olympus. Zeus was the chief god.

- Ancestor worship still survives in parts of Africa and China. People believe the dead look after the living, so they perform ceremonies to their ancestors in the hope they will bring good luck.

Government

To live together in peace, people need to agree on certain rules or **laws**. Each country of the world has a **government** that makes decisions about how a country should be run, and makes the laws for its people. The kind of government varies from one country to another.

Governments collect **taxes**, which is money taken from the wages that people earn. These taxes are used to pay for such things as schools, hospitals, and roads.

Strange but true

- English medieval monks practiced a form of communal government. They owned all their possessions jointly.

- New Zealand was the first country to allow women to vote. This happened in 1893.

- The world's largest election was held in India in 1989. Over 304 million people voted and 3½ million staff were needed to collect the votes.

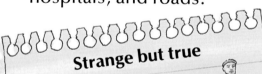

Democracy

Most Western countries are **democracies**. Democracy means:

- "Rule by the people." People vote to choose representatives who take part in the government of the country.

- There is a choice of political parties to elect (vote for).

- There are basic human rights, such as the freedom to criticize the government.

Communism

There have been **communist** governments in Russia, China, Cuba, and parts of Africa. There are few communist countries left. Under communism:

- People can vote, but only for officials of the Communist Party.

- All factories, farms, and stores are owned by the state.

- There is no freedom of speech; no one is allowed to criticize the government or its leaders.

Dictatorship

In a **dictatorship**, one person holds all the power. The people are not allowed to take any part in government or to criticize the leader.

- The Ancient Romans sometimes passed all power to one man — a dictator — in times of war. This ensured that they had a strong leader in a time of trouble. After the war, his power was supposed to end.

- Modern dictators have included Hitler (Germany), Stalin (USSR), Mao Tse-tung (China), Ceausescu (Romania), and Saddam Hussein (Iraq).

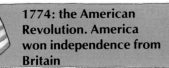 1774: the American Revolution. America won independence from Britain

 1789: the French Revolution. The king was overthrown and a republic set up

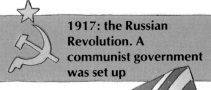 1917: the Russian Revolution. A communist government was set up

Government by parliament

The word **parliament** comes from an old French word meaning "to talk." Parliament is where politicians elected by the people meet to discuss problems and govern the country. The **British parliamentary system** is the oldest in the world:

- The British parliament is divided into the House of Commons and the House of Lords. Members of the House of Lords are not elected.

- King Edward I of England held a parliament in 1295. All later parliaments are based on it.

- Many other countries have parliaments based on the British system.

Houses of Parliament, London

- In Britain the monarch (king or queen) heads the country but is not directly involved in government. Monarchs inherit their titles and are not elected.

Government of the U.S.A.

The United States of America is a **republic** (a country without a king or queen). It is led by an elected **president**.

- Each state has its own local government. The national government in Washington controls all the state governments.

The White House, Washington, D.C., home of the President.

- People vote in elections for the political party they want to govern the country. The leader of the winning party becomes the president.

- There are three branches of government: the Executive, Congress, and the Supreme Court. In this way, power is divided and each branch is able to check the actions of the other two.

- Congress is divided into an upper and lower house — the Senate and the House of Representatives.

The Arts

1820s France: first photograph taken by Joseph Nicéphore Niepce

Human beings express their thoughts and feelings through **art**, by writing stories and plays, drawing, playing music, painting pictures, and making sculptures.

Cave painting

Some arts are very ancient. Prehistoric cave paintings and carvings, ancient Greek poetry, sculptures, and buildings still survive. They show the creativity of people long ago. Today there are also **modern art forms** such as motion pictures, television, and photography.

Literature

Literature is written art. It includes **poetry**, **plays,** and **novels**.

- The oldest poems and stories were told out loud, not written down. They were passed down by memory from one storyteller to another.

- When more people learned to read and write, stories were written down. All books were written and illustrated by hand until printing was invented in the 15th Century.

- The first story books for children were written in the 19th Century. *Swiss Family Robinson* and *Alice in Wonderland* were among the first children's stories ever published.

From left to right: quill pen, fountain pen, typewriter and word processor.

Strange but true

- Decorated bones dug up in Germany may be the most ancient pieces of art ever found. They are about 35,000 years old.

- In 1517, Francis I, King of France, bought the "Mona Lisa" to hang in his bathroom.

- The Globe Theatre in London had no roof. If it rained, performances were cancelled.

- Audiences at the Globe Theatre were noisy and rowdy. Fights often broke out in front of the stage.

Visual arts

Visual arts include **painting**, **drawing,** and **sculpture**.

- Prehistoric people painted pictures of animals and hunters on cave walls. Some have been found that were painted about 25,000 years ago.

- One of the world's best-known paintings is the "Mona Lisa" painted by Leonardo da Vinci between 1503 and 1507. Now it is too valuable to be given a price.

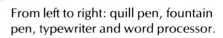

Drama

Plays are stories written for actors to perform. Today they are usually acted in purpose-built **theaters**.

● Ancient Greek plays were performed in open-air theaters. Actors wore masks and took part in plays that told stories about Greek gods and heroes.

● In Europe, about 500 years ago, people watched plays about Bible stories. Actors performed on open carts that could be moved from place to place.

Globe Theatre

Shakespeare

● The world-famous playwright, William Shakespeare, lived in England in the 16th Century. Many of his plays were performed at the Globe Theatre in London.

● The Globe was circular in shape. Rich members of the audience sat on or around the stage. Poor people stood in front of the stage. Women were not allowed to act, so boys played women's parts.

Music

Here are some of the most common groups of **musical instruments**:

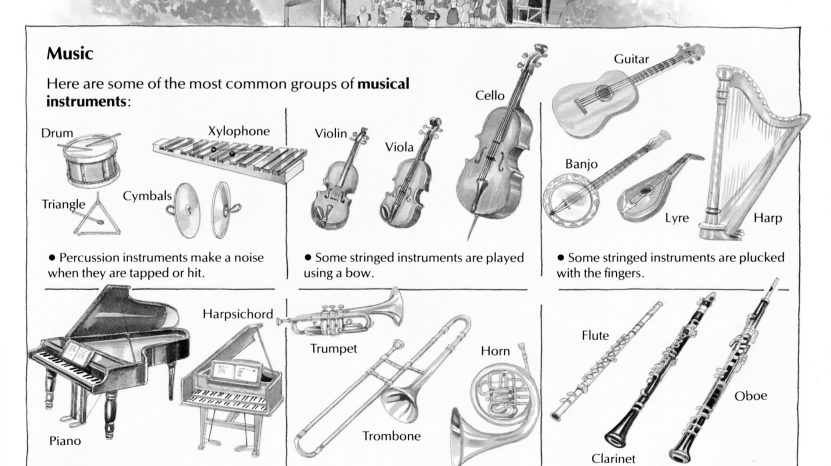

Drum
Xylophone
Triangle
Cymbals

● Percussion instruments make a noise when they are tapped or hit.

Violin
Viola
Cello

● Some stringed instruments are played using a bow.

Guitar
Banjo
Lyre
Harp

● Some stringed instruments are plucked with the fingers.

Harpsichord
Piano

● Keyboard instruments have keys that you press with your fingers. Each key makes a different sound.

Trumpet
Horn
Trombone

● You blow into wind instruments to make music. Some are made of brass.

Flute
Clarinet
Oboe

● Some wind instruments have reeds that you blow into to make a sound.

Famous People

Only a small number of people from the past have become so **famous** that their names are still remembered long after their death. Some of these people became famous for their **daring deeds** and **leadership**. Others are famous for helping to **improve other people's lives**. Many are remembered because the stories of their lives are so **dramatic**. Today, television, motion

pictures, and newspapers can quickly make people famous all over the world. In the past it was difficult to become well known. Here you can find out just a little about some of the most famous people.

Tutankhamun

Tutankhamun was a **pharaoh**, or ruler, of ancient Egypt. He died in 1352 B.C. He has become famous because, more than 3,000 years after his death, his tomb was discovered containing gold, jewels, and many other beautiful objects.

- Tutankhamun became pharaoh when he was 11 years old. He married an Egyptian princess.

- He died when he was about 18.

- In 1922 archaeologists discovered his tomb in Egypt in the Valley of the Kings.

- The pharaoh's body was mummified (preserved and wrapped in bandages) inside a coffin made of solid gold.

Queen Elizabeth I

Queen Elizabeth I lived from 1533 to 1603. She was one of the most famous **rulers of England**. Her court was well known for its poets, painters, musicians, and playwrights.

- Elizabeth was born in 1533, the daughter of King Henry VIII and Anne Boleyn. When Elizabeth was a baby, her father had her mother beheaded.

- When she was a young girl she was locked up for a while in the Tower of London by her half-sister Mary. Mary thought Elizabeth was plotting against her.

- After Mary's death, Elizabeth came to the throne of England. She was 25 and reigned for another 45 years.

Mozart (1756-1791): musical genius who began composing at the age of five

 Queen Victoria (1819-1901): popular and longest-reigning British monarch

 Picasso (1881-1973): Spanish painter who influenced modern art styles

Napoleon Bonaparte

Napoleon, who lived from 1769 to 1821, was a famous French **leader** and **ruler**. He conquered large parts of Europe and made himself emperor over them.

- He was born on the island of Corsica and went to a military school in Paris.

- He became head of the French army and won many victories throughout Europe.

- He reorganized France by improving the law, banks, trade, and education. He also encouraged the sciences and the arts.

- In 1804 he crowned himself Emperor of France. His wife, Josephine, was made Empress.

- When his enemies in Europe invaded France, Napoleon was sent into exile on Elba, an island off the coast of Italy.

- He escaped from Elba and returned to France, gathering an army. However, he was finally beaten at the Battle of Waterloo.

Abraham Lincoln

Abraham Lincoln lived from 1809 to 1865. From a humble background he rose to become the sixteenth **president of the United States**, leading the country at a dramatic point in its history.

- Lincoln grew up as a farmer's son, living in a log cabin in Kentucky. He studied law and began to take an active part in politics.

- In 1860 he was elected President of the United States. The Civil War broke out soon after. Lincoln led the Union generals during the war.

- He worked to change laws and to improve life for all Americans. In particular he brought about the end of slavery in the United States.

- Toward the end of the Civil War, Lincoln was shot dead by a political enemy while at the theater.

Gandhi

Gandhi was an important **Indian leader**. He lived from 1869 to 1948. During his life he worked to bring peace and justice to the world. His ideas and courage made him admired in many countries.

- He was born in India and went to study law in London when he was 19.

- As a lawyer in South Africa and in India he worked to help the poor and suffering, trying to change laws that were unfair.

- Many Indian people called him "Mahatma," which means "great soul."

- He led the Indian people in their struggle for independence from Britain.

- Gandhi believed there was no need to be violent to solve the world's problems. To draw attention to his beliefs he sometimes went on hunger-strikes that endangered his life.

- Shortly after India became independent, Gandhi was shot dead by an enemy at an open-air prayer meeting.

Strange but true

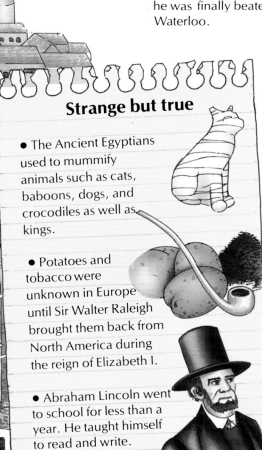

- The Ancient Egyptians used to mummify animals such as cats, baboons, dogs, and crocodiles as well as kings.

- Potatoes and tobacco were unknown in Europe until Sir Walter Raleigh brought them back from North America during the reign of Elizabeth I.

- Abraham Lincoln went to school for less than a year. He taught himself to read and write.

31

Inventions

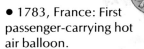

Early humans learned to use simple stone tools over 2 million years ago. Since then people have gradually gathered **knowledge** and **skills**. Now there are many **inventions** that have changed the way people live.

The number of inventions has increased enormously in the 20th Century. People who lived only a hundred years ago would be amazed to see how it is now possible to send messages around the world in seconds, conquer diseases, and even send people to the Moon!

Transportation

Until about 200 years ago, **transportation** was slow, difficult, and uncomfortable. Since that time there have been many changes:

● Late 1700s: Road-building improved, so more people began to travel in horse-drawn coaches.

● 1783, France: First passenger-carrying hot air balloon.

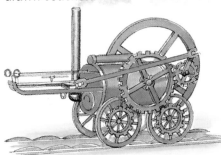

● 1803, Great Britain: Richard Trevithick built the first steam locomotive to pull wagons.

● 1825, Great Britain: First steam public railroad.

● 1885, Germany: First gasoline-driven car.

● 1903, U.S.A.: First powered flight by Orville and Wilbur Wright's airplane, Flyer 1.

● 1950s, worldwide: First jet-engined airliners introduced, able to carry many passengers at high speed.

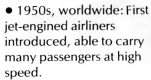

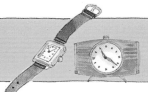

Communications

Ideas spread quickly when they can be easily passed on to other people. These are some important stages in the development of **communications**:

● Paper: In about 3500 B.C. the Egyptians invented paper called papyrus. It was made from reeds. The Chinese invented the modern kind of paper almost 2,000 years ago.

● Printing: In 1450 Johannes Gutenberg of Germany invented a press that could print books easily. Books before this time were copied by hand.

● Telephone: In 1876 the inventor, Alexander Graham Bell, developed the telephone. For the first time people could speak to each other over long distances.

● Radio: In 1894 Guglielmo Marconi experimented with radio waves and used them to send messages without any wires being needed.

● Satellites: In 1957 the first satellite was sent into space by the USSR. Satellites now send telephone and TV signals around the world.

A modern telephone

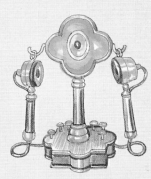

Bell's telephone

Medicine

Here are some important developments in **medicine**:

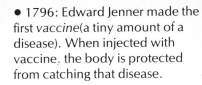

● 1796: Edward Jenner made the first *vaccine* (a tiny amount of a disease). When injected with vaccine, the body is protected from catching that disease.

● 1846: Ether, the first successful *anesthetic*, was used. Anesthetics deaden pain and make surgery safer.

● 1867: Joseph Lister performed the first operation using *antiseptics*. They kill the germs that cause illness. Before their use, many patients died from infections.

● 1895: *X rays* were discovered by Wilhelm Röntgen. X rays are invisible waves of energy that pass through flesh but are absorbed by bone. This allows pictures to be taken of the inside of the body.

● 1939: Penicillin, the first *antibiotic*, was developed. Antibiotics are drugs that kill the bacteria that cause illness.

● 1967: The first heart *transplant* was performed. Transplant operations enable unhealthy organs such as hearts, lungs, or kidneys to be replaced with healthy ones.

Sports and Games

In prehistoric times, as people hunted for food, they learned to run and to throw. The **oldest sports** — running, throwing, archery, and wrestling — grew out of hunting skills. As people began to settle into farming communities, they turned these skills into sports for **exercise** and **amusement**.

Soccer, the world's most popular team game.

Today there are thousands of different sports and games, each with their own **rules**. Some involve just one person testing out his or her skill against another. Some involve teams of people competing against each other. Taking part in games and sports is not only healthy exercise; it is fun, too. Even just being a spectator can be exciting.

The Olympic Games

The first **Olympic Games** were held about 2,700 years ago at the Temple of Zeus, in Olympia, Greece.

- Soldiers in ancient Greece were trained to run, jump, and throw. They competed against each other in the Olympic athletic events.

- Winners of the ancient Games were given an olive branch and treated as national heroes.

- In Ancient Greece the Games were a festival of mind and body, and included poetry and music as well as athletics.

Team games

Many of the world's most **popular sports** involve two **teams** competing against each other. Here are some examples:

- Soccer – Number in team: 11
Ball: round, leather
How ball is moved: kicked
Object: to score goals by kicking the ball into a netted goalmouth

- Football – Number in team: 11
Ball: oval, leather
How ball is moved: carried/thrown
Object: to gain points by carrying ball into endzone or kicking ball over H-shaped posts

- Baseball – Number in team: 9
Ball: small, horse-hide
How ball is moved: hit with long cylindrical wooden bat
Object: to score runs around a diamond-shaped field.

Baseball

- Cricket – Number in team: 11
Ball: small, leather-covered
How ball is moved: hit with flat side of long wooden bat
Object: to score runs between two sets of wooden wickets

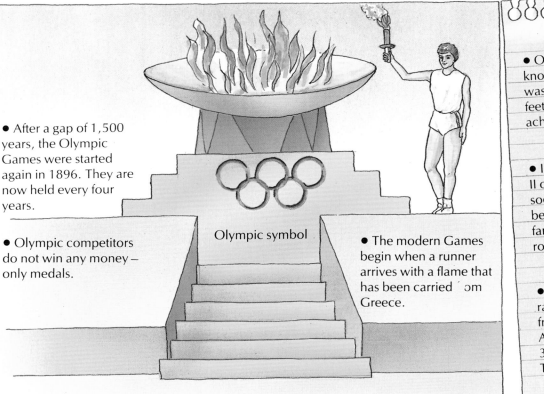

Chess: India,
about A.D. 200

Dominoes: China,
about A.D. 1100

Monopoly: U.S.A.,
1930

• After a gap of 1,500 years, the Olympic Games were started again in 1896. They are now held every four years.

• Olympic competitors do not win any money – only medals.

Olympic symbol

• The modern Games begin when a runner arrives with a flame that has been carried from Greece.

Strange but true

• One of the earliest known Olympic records was a long-jump of 23 feet (7m). It was achieved in about 656 B.C.

• In 1314, King Edward II of England banned soccer in London because the players and fans had become so rowdy.

• The longest running race was held in 1928 from New York to Los Angeles — a distance of 3,422 miles (5,507 km). The winner took 79 days!

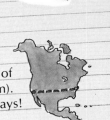

Indoor games

Not all games involve physical strength. Many call for **mental skills**, or rely on **luck**. Here are some of the world's best-known **indoor games**:

• Chess: an ancient strategy game played on a board of 64 black and white squares. Each player has black or white pieces: 1 king, 1 queen, 2 bishops, 2 castles, 2 knights, and 8 pawns.

• Checkers: related to chess but older and simpler. It is played with round counters.

• Ludo, Snakes and Ladders: games of chance relying on luck. Moves of counters are controlled by throwing dice.

• Backgammon: a mixture of chance and skill. Players use a colored board and have 15 counters each. They throw two dice and try to be first to move all their counters round and off the board.

Backgammon

Snakes and Ladders

Chess

• Playing cards: there are many games involving cards. Some are team games (e.g: Bridge). Some can even be played by one person on their own (e.g: Solitaire). Cards come in decks of 52, in four suits: Hearts, Spades, Clubs, and Diamonds.

Limits and Records

There are many **feats of daring** that people have achieved over the centuries. They range from **explorations** of the world's most isolated places to **breaking records** by pushing human skills to the limit.

New records are being set all the time as humans strive to break barriers of endurance and achievement.

Human heights

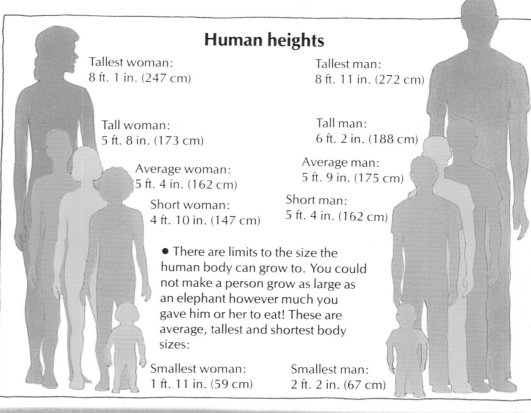

Tallest woman:
8 ft. 1 in. (247 cm)

Tallest man:
8 ft. 11 in. (272 cm)

Tall woman:
5 ft. 8 in. (173 cm)

Tall man:
6 ft. 2 in. (188 cm)

Average woman:
5 ft. 4 in. (162 cm)

Average man:
5 ft. 9 in. (175 cm)

Short woman:
4 ft. 10 in. (147 cm)

Short man:
5 ft. 4 in. (162 cm)

• There are limits to the size the human body can grow to. You could not make a person grow as large as an elephant however much you gave him or her to eat! These are average, tallest and shortest body sizes:

Smallest woman:
1 ft. 11 in. (59 cm)

Smallest man:
2 ft. 2 in. (67 cm)

Exploring the world

Some people have been prepared to risk their lives and suffer great discomfort to be the first **explorers**. Here are some famous achievements of exploration:

• A Norwegian team first reached the South Pole in 1911 after a 53-day march.

• The first polar round-the-world trip began in 1979 in London. The explorers traveled to the South Pole, the North Pole, and back to London, a distance of 35,000 miles (56,325 km). They reached home in 1982.

• On July 21, 1969, U.S. astronaut Neil Armstrong became the first person to walk on the Moon.

• The longest recorded swim was 1,826 miles (2938 km) down the Mississippi River in 1930. The swimmer spent 742 hours in the water.

• The first people to climb Mount Everest, the highest mountain in the world, were Edmund Hillary and Tenzing Norgay, in 1953.

Heights and depths

Modern technology has enabled people to reach the depths of the **ocean** and the heights of **space**.

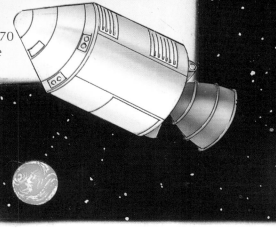

- Apollo 13 astronauts reached a height of 248,670 miles (400,187 km) above the Earth.

- The highest a hot-air balloon has flown is 113,740 ft. (34,668 m) over the Gulf of Mexico in 1961.

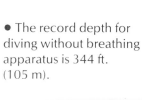

- The record depth for diving without breathing apparatus is 344 ft. (105 m).

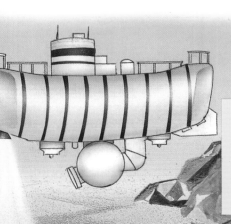

- The furthest anyone has reached into the sea depths is 35,814 ft. (10,916 m), inside a submersible craft exploring the Pacific Ocean.

Strange but true

- The human brain is five times smaller than an adult elephant's brain.

- The record for balancing on one foot with no support is 34 hours.

- A baby's head is about a quarter of its total body length. An adult's head is only about one eighth of its total height.

Human limits

There are many things humans cannot do as well as some animals can:

- They are not as fast as cheetahs, which can run at 62 mph (100 km/h).

- They are not as strong as a rhinoceros beetle, which can carry 850 times its own weight on its back.

- They cannot smell as well as the Emperor moth, which can detect smells 7 miles (11 km) away.

- They cannot hear as well as dolphins and bats, which can hear sounds too high-pitched for humans to hear.

- They cannot eat as much as the Polyphemus moth, which eats 86,000 times its own birth weight in 48 hours.

- They cannot make as much noise as South American howler monkeys, whose cries can be heard 10 miles (16 km) away.

Through the ages, people have waged **wars** and committed **crimes**. This negative side of human nature is often caused by greed for money, property, or power. Sometimes, though, people have been driven by poverty and injustice to be violent or break the law.

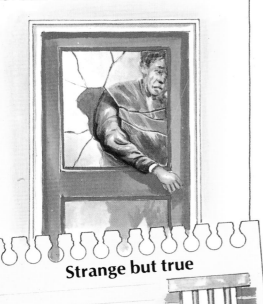

Weapons

Warfare has changed over the centuries. Here are some of the **weapons** people have invented to defend themselves and attack others:

• Hand weapons are used for stabbing or hitting. They are the oldest group of weapons, and include clubs, swords, and spears.

• Catapults are early examples of shooting weapons. Guns and cannon came later. Modern versions include machine guns, torpedoes, and guided missiles.

• The first bombs, used in the 16th Century, were hollow metal balls filled with gunpowder. They were lit with a fuse.

• Booby trap weapons probably originated from animal-trapping methods. Modern booby traps include landmines that explode when touched.

• Modern bombs include the devastating nuclear bomb, which can poison the atmosphere with radiation.

Strange but true

• The longest jail sentence passed was in the United States — 10,000 years for a triple murder.

• The shortest war on record lasted for just 38 minutes on August 27, 1896. It was fought between the United Kingdom and Zanzibar (now Tanzania).

• China has the largest army in the world, with over 2 million soldiers.

Wars

Wars have been waged throughout history. Here are some facts about **warfare**:

• In the last 5,500 years there have been only 292 years when no known war was being fought somewhere in the world.

• The longest war was fought between England and France. It lasted 115 years, from 1338 to 1453.

• World War II (1939-45) cost approximately $1.5 trillion. That is more than all the world's previous wars put together.

• World War II also saw the greatest loss of life of any war. About 54 million people died.

• It is estimated that in 1988 the amount spent on weapons throughout the world was $660 billion.

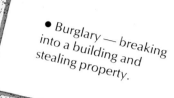
Crime

All societies have **laws**. **Crimes** are acts that are forbidden and are punished by law. Here are some major crimes:

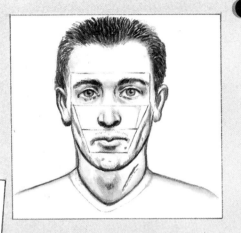

- Arson — purposely setting fire to a building or other property.

- Assault — hurting someone physically.

- Murder — killing someone intentionally. Manslaughter is different from murder. It means killing someone by accident or in self-defense.

- Burglary — breaking into a building and stealing property.

- Treason — helping the enemies of your country, or (in some places) attacking the ruler of your country.

Punishment

A person found guilty of a crime is punished. This is intended to **stop them offending** again, and to **discourage other people** from committing crimes. Here are some methods of **punishment**:

- Imprisonment: Criminals are locked in jail, away from society.

- Community service: Offenders are not imprisoned, but they are made to work for the community.

- Fines: Offenders pay for their crimes by handing over a sum of money.

- Probation: Offenders are not imprisoned but their behavior is regularly checked by officials called probation officers.

- Death penalty: In China, South Africa, Turkey, Iran, Saudi Arabia, Malaysia, 36 states of the U.S., and the former USSR; murderers are put to death.

- In Australia and Britain the death penalty has been kept for those who commit treason.

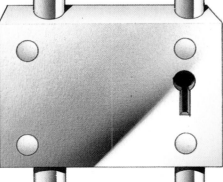

The Future

Life on Earth has changed more during the last hundred years than at any other time since people lived on the planet. It is impossible to know what further changes will happen in the future, but it is clear there will be great **challenges** to meet.

One of the greatest challenges will be to preserve life on the planet from **pollution**. Ways will have to be found, too, of sharing out the **world's resources** more fairly.

Pollution

Pollution of the **environment** is threatening the world's water and air. International laws, together with conservation efforts by everyone, can help to limit the damage.

● The build-up of carbon dioxide gas in the Earth's atmosphere has resulted in global warming — the slow warming up of the air temperature.

● Acid rain contains poisonous substances leaked from factories and cars. It can quickly destroy plantlife.

● CFC gases (used in spray aerosols and refrigerators) seem to be damaging the Earth's ozone layer, a blanket of gas about 15 miles (25 km) above the ground.

● Oceans and rivers are sometimes polluted by poisonous industrial waste that can kill fish and affect drinking water. Many countries now have laws to limit this pollution.

● Carbon dioxide is released by burning fossil fuels such as coal, gas, and oil. It also increases when forests are destroyed, because trees use up the carbon dioxide.

Saving animals and plants

The actions of people have put many **animals** and **plants** in danger of **extinction**, which means that they may die out altogether. World organizations and governments are working to stop this continuing.

● Some of the world's rarest plant species are known by only one specimen.

● Each year an area of rain forest about the size of Switzerland disappears. The trees are cut for wood or cleared for mining or farming.

● An animal is declared extinct if it has not been seen for 50 years.

Extinct dodo

 **Insulate houses so they need less heating**

 **Plant more trees**

 **Use more buses and trains so the number of cars can be reduced**

New sources of power

The world's supplies of coal, gas, and oil are being used up rapidly as cities and industries develop. In the future, people may learn how to use **new sources of power** that do not run out:

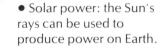

- Wind power: electricity can be generated by using windmills that turn simply by the power of the wind.

- Water power: experiments are taking place to find out how to use the power of the world's oceans and rivers to produce electricity.

- New fuels: these can be made from tiny algae plants, from alcohol, and even from animal dung.

- Solar power: the Sun's rays can be used to produce power on Earth.

- Nuclear fusion: by joining atoms together, enormous amounts of power could be generated. This would be safer than the atomic power in use now.

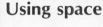
Using space

Space could be a very useful **resource**. Here are some possible future developments:

- Raw materials such as iron ore could be mined on the Moon.

- Giant solar power stations could orbit the Earth, sending down power gathered from the Sun.

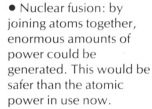

A space station being built

- People may be able to live in space, on space stations orbiting the Earth.

People Facts and Lists

Early people

These are the approximate dates when scientists believe our human ancestors lived:

Australopithecus: 1-8 million years ago
Homo Habilis: 1.5-2.5 million years ago
Homo Erectus: 300,000-1.6 million years ago
Homo Sapiens: first appeared 1.6 million years ago
Neanderthal people: 35,000-100,000 years ago
Modern people: first appeared 30,000-50,000 years ago

Prehistoric remains of early people

Here are some of the most important prehistoric finds made by anthropologists:

Year found	Find	Where found	Dating from (years ago)
1856	Neanderthal skull and bones	Germany	120,000
1868	Cromagnon skeleton (Homo Sapiens)	France	35,000
1924	Australopithecus skull	Botswana	1 million
1974	Australopithecus skeleton (Lucy)	Ethiopia	3-4 million
1975	Homo Erectus skull	Kenya	1.5 million
1980	Homo Sapiens	Tanzania	120,000

● Anthropologists who discovered the oldest Australopithecine skeleton called her Lucy after the Beatles song "Lucy in the Sky with Diamonds."

● Lucy died around 3 million years ago. She was about 40 years old when she died and only 3 ft. 6 in. (106 cm) tall.

Population

These are some of the most crowded countries in the world:

Country	People per square mile in 1990
Monaco	38,024
Singapore	11,360
Vatican City	6,500
Malta	2,904
Bangladesh	2,038
Bahrain	1,887
Maldives	1,867
Barbados	1,555
Taiwan	1,459
Mauritius	1,375

Some of the least crowded countries in the world are:

Country	People per square mile in 1990
Greenland	0.3
Western Sahara	1.3
Mongolia	3.6
Mauritania	5.0
Australia	5.7
Botswana	5.7
Libya	6.2
Surinam	6.5
Canada	7.5
Iceland	8.3

● There are 68 people per square mile in the United States.

The human body

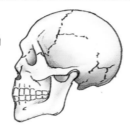

● Most people spend about a third of their lives asleep.

● A two-year-old child is about half the height it will reach as an adult.

● The heart beats about 70 times a minute. That is nearly 37 million times a year!

● The longest and strongest bone in the body is the femur, or thigh bone.

● There are 639 muscles in the human body.

● There are four basic blood groups found throughout the world. They are called A, AB, B, and O. Group O is the most common.

● Some people have such good color vision that they can tell the difference between as many as 300,000 different shades of color.

● The human ear can pick out more than 1,500 different musical tones.

● It is impossible to sneeze with your eyes open!

People of the world

● Scientists who study the way the world's peoples are related to each other study the following, which can vary from group to group:

Skin
Hair
Language
Skeleton
Blood group
Color blindness
Type of ear wax
Inherited diseases

Languages

These are the most widely spoken of the world's 5,000 languages:

Language	Number of speakers
Mandarin Chinese	788 million
English	420 million
Hindustani	300 million
Spanish	296 million
Russian	285 million

- Other widely spoken languages include Arabic, Portuguese, Bengali, German, and Japanese. They each have about 100-200 million speakers.

- The American and English languages are similar but not exactly the same. Here are some differences:

American English	English
Candy	Sweets
Check	Cheque
Checkers	Draughts
Biscuit	Bread roll or scone
Cookie	Biscuit
Closet	Cupboard
Diaper	Nappy
Drugstore	Chemist's shop
Elevator	Lift
Fall	Autumn
Faucet	Tap
First floor	Ground floor
Gasoline	Petrol
Purse	Handbag
Row house	Terrace house
Sidewalk	Pavement
Skillet	Frying pan
Suspenders	Braces
Thumbtack	Drawing pin
Undershirt	Vest
Vest	Waistcoat

Food

The energy content of food is measured in calories. This is how many calories some foods contain:

Food	Number of calories in 3½ ounces (100 grams)
Butter	740
White sugar	394
Wholewheat bread	318
White bread	233
Rice (boiled)	123
Potatoes (boiled)	80
Milk (non-skimmed)	65
Apple (raw)	46
Peas	41
Cabbage (boiled)	9

- An adult man needs an average of 3,000 calories a day. A woman needs about 2,200.

This is how many calories per day most people get, on average, in some countries of the world:

Country	Number of calories/day
U.S.A.	3,600
Australia	3,300
Brazil	2,600
China	2,600
India	2,200
Chad (Africa)	1,700

This is how many calories some activities use up:

Activity	Calories used per hour
Resting in bed	60
Driving a car	168
Washing dishes	230
Walking at 3.5 mph (6 km/h)	492
Cycling at 13 mph (21 km/h)	660
Running at 5 mph (8 km/h)	850
Swimming breaststroke at 56 strokes/min	1212

Clothes

These are some traditional clothes from around the world:

Clothing	Worn by Men/Women	Country
Aba – long robe	M	Nigeria
Dhoti – white cotton loincloth	M	India
Fustanella – pleated kilt	M	Greece, Turkey
Kaftan – long loose robe	M	Middle East and North Africa
Kilt – pleated skirt in the special colors of a family, or clan	M/W	Scotland
Kimono – long loose robe with wide sleeves and a sash	W	Japan
Parka – fur-lined padded coat	M/W	Arctic, Alaska
Poncho – cloak made of a blanket with a hole to put the head through	M/W	Mexico, South and Central America
Sari – long, wide strip of decorated cloth worn wrapped around the body and often also over the head	W	India
Sarong – decorated strip of cloth wrapped around the body	M/W	Far East

- In China, in the past, only wealthy people were allowed to wear yellow. Most people wore blue, because the blue dye was cheap.

- Traditionally, Chinese brides wore red. White was the color for funerals.

- Levi Strauss made the first pair of blue jeans in 1850. They were intended as work trousers for American miners looking for gold.

- In Ancient Rome only important people wore purple clothes. This is because the purple dye came from a particular kind of shellfish and was very expensive.

People Facts and Lists

Religion

These are the world's most popular religions:

Religion	Number of followers
Christianity	1,758 million
Islam	935 million
Hinduism	705 million
Buddhism	303 million
Sikhism	18 million
Judaism	17 million

● 233 million people throughout the world describe themselves as atheists (who do not accept any god) and a further 866 million people describe themselves as non-religious.

Government

British Kings and Queens

These are the most recent British monarchs:

George I	1714-1727
George II	1727-1760
George III	1760-1820
George IV	1820-1830
William IV	1830-1837
Victoria	1837-1901
Edward VII	1901-1910
George V	1910-1936
Edward VIII	1936 (abdicated)
George VI	1937-1952
Elizabeth II	1952-

U.S. Presidents

These are the first five Presidents of the United States of America:

President	Years in office
George Washington	1789-1797
John Adams	1797-1801
Thomas Jefferson	1801-1809
James Madison	1809-1817
James Monroe	1817-1825

and the most recent Presidents:

President	Years in office
John F. Kennedy	1961-1963
Lyndon Johnson	1963-1969
Richard Nixon	1969-1974
Gerald Ford	1974-1977
James Carter	1977-1981
Ronald Reagan	1981-1990
George Bush	1990-

Ten famous children's books

Hans Christian Andersen	Fairy Tales (including *The Emperor's New Clothes*)
J. M. Barrie	Peter Pan
Lewis Carroll	Alice's Adventures in Wonderland
Roald Dahl	The BFG
Rudyard Kipling	The Jungle Book
A. A. Milne	Winnie-the-Pooh
Beatrix Potter	The Tale of Peter Rabbit
R. L. Stevenson	Treasure Island
Mark Twain	The Adventures of Huckleberry Finn
E. B. White	Charlotte's Web

Ten great writers

Here is a list of ten great writers and one of their best-known works:

Jane Austen	Pride and Prejudice
Emily Bronte	Wuthering Heights
Miguel de Cervantes	Don Quixote
Geoffrey Chaucer	Canterbury Tales
Dante	Divine Comedy
Charles Dickens	Great Expectations
Dostoevsky	Crime and Punishment
Gustave Flaubert	Madame Bovary
Herman Melville	Moby Dick
Tolstoy	War and Peace

Painters

These are some of the world's famous painters:

Artist	Dates	Nationality	Major subjects
Sandro Botticelli	1444-1510	Italian	Religious pictures
Pieter Brueghel	1520-1569	Flemish	Pictures of village life
John Constable	1776-1837	English	English landscapes
Leonardo da Vinci	1452-1519	Italian	Mona Lisa
Paul Gauguin	1848-1903	French	People and landscapes of Tahiti, South Pacific
Michelangelo	1475-1564	Italian	Religious pictures on the Sistine chapel ceiling, Vatican City
Claude Monet	1840-1926	French	Impressionist pictures
Pablo Picasso	1881-1973	Spanish	Many styles, including Cubism that changed modern art completely
Rembrandt	1606-1669	Dutch	Portraits
Joseph Turner	1775-1851	English	Landscapes
Vincent Van Gogh	1853-1890	Dutch	Landscapes, people, and everyday objects

Ten famous composers

Composer	Dates	Nationality
Bach	1685-1750	German
Beethoven	1770-1827	German
Brahms	1833-1897	German
Britten	1913-1976	English
Chopin	1810-1849	Polish
Gershwin	1898-1937	American
Haydn	1732-1809	Austrian
Mozart	1756-1791	Austrian
Stravinsky	1882-1971	Russian
Tchaikovsky	1840-1893	Russian

Cinema

● The first film with sound, called a "talking picture," was *The Jazz Singer*, made in 1927.

● The world's largest motion-picture theater complex is in Brussels, Belgium. It has 24 screens and seats 7,000 people.

● The world's largest motion-picture theater is Radio City Music Hall, in New York City. It has 5,874 seats.

Inventions

These are the approximate dates when some important discoveries were made:

Invention	When	Where
Pottery	7000 B.C.	Iran
Bricks	6000 B.C.	Jericho
Writing	4000 B.C.	Mesopotamia
The wheel	3200 B.C.	Mesopotamia
Glass	3000 B.C.	Egypt
Printing	770 B.C.	Japan
Gunpowder	A.D. 950	China

These modern objects were invented a surprisingly long time ago:

Knitting machine	1589
Microscope	1590
Thermometer	1592
Submarine	1620
Adding machine	1623
Pressure cooker	1679
Machine gun	1718
Lightning rod	1752
Parachute	1783
Battery	1800
Burglar alarm	1858

Around the world

These are the times it took various craft to go round the world:

1500s   Sailing ship   2 years

1929   Airship   21 days 7 hr

1957   Boeing B-52   1 day 21 hrs

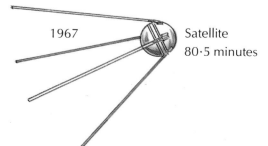

1967   Satellite   80·5 minutes

Conflict and crime

● The number of prisoners in the United States at the end of 1990 reached a record high of 77,243.

● A survey in 1986 showed that more than 8 people per 100,000 in the U.S.A. were murdered that year. That was twice as many as in the next highest countries in the survey — Hungary, Israel, and Australia. Norway had the fewest murders.

● During World War I, more than a million soldiers were killed or wounded at the first Battle of the Somme in 1916.

● About 2.5 million people died at the Battle of Stalingrad in 1942-43, fought between the Germans and the Russians during World War II.

● In all, about 55 million people were killed during World War II. Almost a half of these people were from the USSR.

These countries fought each other in the two World Wars:

War	Dates	Won by	Against
World War 1	1914-18	Belgium, Britain and the Empire, France, Italy, Japan, Russia, Serbia, U.S.A.	Austria-Hungary, Bulgaria, Germany, Ottoman Empire
World War II	1939-45	Australia, Belgium, Britain, Canada, China, Denmark, France, Greece, Netherlands, New Zealand, Norway, Poland, South Africa, U.S.A., USSR, Yugoslavia	Bulgaria, Finland, Germany, Hungary, Italy, Japan, Romania

Olympic Games

● The first recorded Olympic Games were held in 776 B.C., although they were probably held for many years before this.

● The ancient Games included running, jumping, wrestling, discus throwing, boxing, and chariot racing.

● The first modern Games, held in 1896, had only 311 competitors, of whom 230 were from Greece.

These were the top medal-winning countries in the 1988 Olympic Games:

Country	Gold	Silver	Bronze
USSR	55	31	46
E. Germany	37	35	30
U.S.A.	36	31	27
W. Germany	11	14	15
Bulgaria	10	12	13
S. Korea	12	10	11

Miscellany

● A scientist has calculated that about 60 billion people died between the years 40,000 B.C. and 1990. This means that about 9 percent of all people who have ever lived are alive today!

● If the age of the Earth (4.6 billion years) is likened to a single year, the following events take place on 31 December, the last day of the year:

4.15 pm: Appearance of humanlike beings

11.10 pm: Arrival of earliest inhabitants in Europe

14 seconds before midnight: Birth of Christ

● Using this same comparison, the life span of someone who lived to be 120 years old would be just three-fourths of a second.

INDEX